STRATEGIC VISION OF MUSTAFA KEMAL ATATURK

I. INTRODUCTION

In order to express the strategic vision of Ataturk, I would like to explain the position of Turkey at the beginning of the Turkish Independence War in 1919.

The Ottoman empire collapsed after World War I. At that time , most critical parts of the country were occupied by British, French, Italian and Greek armies. The Ottoman armies had been discharged, arms and ammunition had been taken, and all transportation systems were controlled by the entente countries. The Sultan had no ability to do anything other than accept what the entente countries dictated to him. Everybody had lost hope and no one knew what to do, except Ataturk. Finally, he made a decision to take the responsibility for the people and create a new state. This state dedicated itself to the sovereignty of the national will. After this decision, on May 19, 1919, he landed in the Black Sea port of Samsun to start the war of independence and he accomplished his plan step by step. He used all his strategic leadership abilities to convince, motivate, and organize the people to overcome all difficulties.

His first message to the people was; "this nation has never lived without independence, we cannot and shall not live without it. In that case there are two alternatives; either independence or death."

In defiance of the Sultan's government, he rallied a liberation army in Anatolia and covened the congress of Erzurum and Sivas where he established the basis for the new national effort under his leadership. On April 23, 1920, the Turkish grand national assembly was inaugurated and Ataturk was elected to its presidency.[1]

During the Turkish Independence War, he repelled the invading enemy forces on the east, on the south and on the west. At the end of August 1922, the Turkish armies won their ultimate victory. On July 24, 1923, the Laussane treaty was signed with the United Kingdom, France, Greece, Italy and others. On the October 29, 1923, the republic was proclaimed and Ataturk was elected president of the Turkish Republic.

The other most important strategic vision of Ataturk was, understanding the importance of western civilization and starting to build a new modern Republic of Turkey.

II. STRATEGIC DECISIONS OF ATATURK

Seeing the position of Ottoman empire, Ataturk made a lot of important decisions and successfully applied all of them. They are as follows:

a. Goals of Ataturk;

(1) The establishment of a national state.

In the beginning of the National Liberation movement, Mustafa Kemal's major goal was the liberation of the country from foreign occupation and the establishment, within national boundaries, of a Turkish state which would be master of its own fate. The notion of a "national Turkish State" was first conceived of during this struggle.[2]

(2) Complete Independence.

Complete independence was naturally a matter of Ataturk's foreign policy particularly concerned with the period of the War of Liberation. Because of foreign intervention, privileges granted to foreigners and the capitulations, the Ottoman Empire in its last years had, to a large extent, lost its independence. Following its defeats, the last Turkish state was in a position of being completely erased from the map. This was the reason for Ataturk's initiation for the War of National Liberation. This goal was stated in the following terms; "In order to render possible our national and economic development and to succeed in achieving orderly administration, like all states, we must possess absolute independence and freedom in the achievement of our development. For this reason, we are opposed to all limitations on our political, judicial, or financial development in the settling of our assessed debts. There shall be no change in this matter.

By complete independence we mean, of course, complete economic, financial, judicial, military, cultural independence and freedom in all matters. Being deprived of independence and freedom in any of these matters is equivalent to the nation's and country's being deprived of all of its independence."[3]

(3) Westernization.

Turkey's western-inclined foreign policy began in Ataturk's time in conjunction with westernization, or more correctly modernization efforts in the cultural sphere. It encountered various obstacles. The modernization process has tried to overcome these obstacles, and partial success has been achieved; consequently, Turkey has slowly but steadily turned toward the west.

Ataturk knew that Turkey's future lay with the West. Therefore, he channeled Turkey toward this general political direction and he expressed the view that Turkey must undergo westernization in order to take its rightful place in the civilized world, as follows:

> "The Turks are the friends of all civilized nations. On condition that they do us no harm and do not interfere with our liberties, foreigners shall always be welcome in our country. Our goal is rapprochement, the re-establishment of bonds with other nations. There are many nations, but there is only one civilization. For the advancement of a nation, it must be a part of this one civilization. The downfall of the Ottoman Empire began on the day that it haughtily severed its ties

4

with European nations because of its military victories against them. This was a mistake which we shall not repeat.

In keeping with our policies, our traditions and our interests, we are inclined to the establishment of a European Turkey, or to be more precise, a Turkey inclined toward the West."[4]

He did as he said. In the Ataturk period, Turkey's western-directed foreign policy was carried out in conjunction with the establishment of cultural ties with the West.

b. Main principals of Ataturk.

(1) Realism.

While determining the basic principles of Turkey's foreign policy, Ataturk always kept in mind both national and international realities. Because of this realistic foreign policy, Turkey was able to both win and preserve its independence. Ataturk's "pacifism" was based on neither concession nor compromises. Just as he never placed the vital interests of the country in danger, he never made any concessions with regard to these interests.

Ataturk's realism prevented him from following a policy of compromise in relations with his country's enemies, and prevented him from being impractical in dealing with all matters.

As a state which was defeated in World War I, if Turkey had acted emotionally, out of a primitive notion of nationalism, it would have been natural for her to join the bloc of nations opposed to the status quo. But Ataturk, who had taken the responsibility of determining the general direction of Turkey's foreign policy, accepted the borders as declared in the National Pact, and avoided leading the country down the path of adventurism.

His statement after the Treaty of Laussanne clearly reveals this fact:

> "It would be naive to believe that the peace we have achieved will be eternal. This is such an important fact that to lose sight of it for even one moment could put the existence of the nation in danger. Certainly as long as others show respect to our law, our honor, and our dignity, we shall not fail to reciprocate, however, we have learned through our bitter experiences that there is little or no respect for the law of those who are weak. It is for this reason that we must not fail to take immediate precautions against all potential dangers."[5]

(2) Allegiance to legality.

It means to obey international rules, agreements and treaties. It is possible to offer a great number of examples of the allegiance to legality in Ataturk's foreign policy. The Montreal signing in 1936, even today in force, is a good example.

(3) Peace at home peace in the world.

When we think of Ataturk's foreign policy, the first of his statements that comes to mind is the often-repeated "Peace at home peace in the world." During the war of national liberation a perfect balance was established between resources and the interests of the country. With The National Pact drawing the countries boundaries, Ataturk accepted the entire people living within these boundaries as Turkish, on condition these people accepted themselves that they were Turks. This was the first step toward peace at home.

In fact, Turkey's adopting the principle of "peace at home peace in the world" as the basis of its foreign policy occurred at the very same time that new blocks were beginning to be formed in the international arena. Taking this principle as its watchword, Turkey attempted to maintain good relations with all states, but established closer ties with non-belligerent states in their opposition to those states which were attempting to destroy international peace. The fact that the Soviet Union, which was threatened in the west by Germany in the east by Japan, had established good relations with Great Britain and France made it easier for Turkey, too, to follow a policy of establishing good relations with those two states.

Turkey did not have the power to influence international policy with respect to the preservation of peace in Europe and the rest of the world. On the other hand, Ataturk believed that if Turkey could establish relations based on equality with Balkan and Near Eastern states which the Ottoman empire had ruled for centuries, this could have a significant effect on the formation of European policy. However, Ataturk realized that this could only come into being if friendly relations were established among the Balkan states. Consequently, from Turkey's efforts on this matter emerged the Balkan Union, with four Balkan states, Turkey, Greece, Yugoslavia and Romania participating.

On the other hand, the abolition of the Caliphate and the foundation of a secular state, as well as the development of a new Turkish nationalism and the westernization efforts of Republican Turkey, gave rise to displeasure with Turkey among the Arab states and other Muslim countries. However, aside from these emotional reasons, there were no important disputed borders or vitally important conflicts of economic and political interests between Turkey and these states. The few social disputes which did exist were not difficult to solve.

Ataturk attempted to develop relations with these countries, just as he had with the west. The good developing relations between Turkey , Iran, Afghanistan, and Iraq led the way to the signing of the Saadabad pact on July 8, 1937. This was not a military alliance, but a pact of friendship and solidarity.[6]

The terms of pact called for non-interference in the internal affairs of the participating states, respect for common boundaries, and mutual guarantees of non-aggression. Thus, by establishing good relations with her western neighbors through the Balkan Pact, and with her eastern neighbors through the Saadabad Pact, Turkey clearly demonstrated that she made no claims on former Ottoman territories, and wanted "peace in the world."

c. Some important orders of Ataturk.

Ataturk made a lot of important decisions and gave a lot of orders, but four of them are emphasized his strategic vision which are as follows:

(1) First order;

"I am not ordering to you to attack, I am ordering to you to die!"[7]
This order was given by Ataturk on April 25, 1915, at Conkbayiri, Canakkale(Dardanelles). At that time the enemy made an attack with 8 battalions and Ataturk wanted a counter attack with 5 battalions.

(2) Second order;

Withdraw order.
This order was given by Ataturk on July 18,1921, at Sakarya. At that time Turkish army was newly established but, the Greek army was powerful and Greek attacks were successful. In this position Ataturk ordered the withdrawal of the Turkish army to the east side of the Sakarya river.

(3) Third order;

"There is no line to defend, there is an area to defend, this area is all the motherland."[8]
This order was given by Ataturk, in the Turkish National Grand Assembly when some members criticized the withdrawal of the army to the eastern side of Sakarya.

(4) Fourth order;

"Armies, your first target is The Mediterranean, Go ahead."[9]

This order was given by Ataturk, on August, 26, 1922, in Ankara, to start the great attack of the Turkish army against the Greek army.

d. Declaration by Ataturk to Turkish youth.

Establishing the Republic of Turkey, Ataturk entrusted it to the Turkish youth. This declaration summarized the strategic vision of Ataturk, and it is as follows;

"Turkish youth! Your first duty is forever to preserve and to defend the Turkish independence and the Turkish Republic.

This is the very foundation of your existence and your future. This foundation is your most precious treasure.

In the future, too, there may be malevolent people at home and abroad who will wish to deprive you of this treasure. If some day you are compelled to defend your independence and your republic, you must not tarry to weigh the possibilities and circumstances of the situation before taking up your duty. These possibilities and circumstances may turn out to be extremely unfavorable. The enemies conspiring against your independence and your republic, may have behind them a victory unprecedented in the annals of the world. It may be that, by violence and ruse, all the fortresses for your beloved fatherland may be captured, all its shipyards occupied, all its armies dispersed and every part of the country invaded. And sadder and graver than all these circumstances, those who hold power within the country may be in error, misguided and may even be traitors. Furthermore, they may identify their personal interests with the political designs of the invaders. The country may be impoverished, ruined and exhausted. Youth of Turkey's future! Even in such circumstances it is your duty to save the Turkish independence and Republic. You will find the strength you need in your noble blood."[10]

III. REVOLUTIONS OF ATATURK

The scope and full meaning of Ataturk's Revolutions can be better appreciated if conditions in Turkey 74 years ago are kept in mind. Between the years 1918 and 1923, Ataturk led the war of independence. Afterwards, in the country where the Ottoman's Sultans had ruled for centuries, as God's Shadow on Earth, he tried to liquidate the old and religious institutions of the Ottoman Empire and lay the foundation of new Turkish State.

a. A National State:

Ataturk had successfully realized the first step of his program was to create a national sovereign and independent state. The Ottoman Empire consisted of many different nations; most of them didn't have the Turkish spirit. Ataturk knew that and drew the frontier of real Turkey- the land inhabited by Turks; beyond these frontiers he would not go. He realized that progress, the well-being, and happiness of his people were more important to the foundation of a new Turkish state.

The idea of independent land within its own national boundaries had already been achieved before 1922; the idea of the real modern state, which was based on the peoples' sovereignty. The principles and general lines of a real national policy and the ability to make these known to the whole population of the country, were developed over a long period of time, making use of all means available and by applying the most rational methods.

Ataturk took the first step toward these goals and abolished the Sultanate, with its centuries of tradition and corruption, and announced that "The Turkish State is a Republic" on October 23, 1923.

b. Secularism:

The abolition of Sultanate was immediately followed by the abolition of the Caliphate in 1924. That meant there would not be any formal religious ties with other Muslim countries anymore. This abolition naturally necessitated the liquidation of all the theocratic institutions on which the Caliphate was based. In a similar way of thinking, the medreses, (theocratic schools,) were closed, and all the theological institutions standing between the individual and the society were suppressed

The next logical step, though one considered unthinkable in those days, was the separation of religion from state affairs. The law of the Koran was entrenched in Turkey and dominated all segments of Turkish society and state. Ataturk proclaimed that the new Turkish State was to be secular, and by virtue of an amendment brought to the constitution, the principle of laicism, so important for the life of the country, was introduced as one of the basic principles of the new democratic and republican constitution.

Afterwards, he replaced the Sheriat, the law of the Koran, with a modern civil code, adapted from the Swiss civil code; a penal code adopted from the Italian Penal Code; a commercial code; and an obligation code. The new legal system was based on Roman Law (1925-1926).[11]

c. The Revolution of Education.

The success of every modernization movement is dependent on success in the field of education. Since Ataturk believed that development would be achieved under the leadership of reason and science, it was inevitable that he would place great importance on national education.

There was a great need for genuinely enlightened people who would approach all of Turkey's problems in a rational way with respect for scientific facts. It was imperative that all Turkish children, girls and boys, peasants and city-dwellers alike, be given the opportunity to have a modern and adequate basic education. It was necessary that the masses be educated more rapidly and more effectively by taking advantage of all the means provided by modern educational technology.

And Ataturk took another vital step to begin the educational revolution; he abolished the use of Arabic script and adopted Latin characters in 1928. Turkish intellectuals had known for a long time that Arabic script was not suitable for the Turkish language. It was very difficult for Turks to master this script and this, in turn, accounted for the high illiteracy rate. But, in the face of strong conservatism, no one had dared to suggest a change; Ataturk determined that.

In a similar way of thinking, the medreses, the theological educational institutions, were closed and a modern education system was built, and the principle of unification of education was applied instead.[12]

   d. Other Revolutions.

As a consequence of this new disposition toward modernization, all laws, regulations, institutions, and methods of a theological nature governing the state organs and social life were abandoned and a variety of socio-political revolutions were introduced, taking into consideration the national realities and exigencies for coherence revolutions introduced, preceding the westernization movement.

   (1) Women's Rights.

Efforts were made toward modernizing women's attire, women's rights secured by the new civil code, systematic measures taken to elevate the cultural status of Turkish mothers, giving women the right to work in almost all professions, granting women suffrage and the right to vote, and to be elected to parliament. Thus, Turkish women gained complete equality in every sense of the word.[13]

   (2) Adoption of International Calendar and Time.

International numerals were put to use, in place of the Islamic system of reckoning whereby clocks are set at 12 every evening at sunset, and the international system based on Greenwich Mean Time was adopted.[14]

(3) Adoption of International Units of Measure.

Complicated units and systems of weight and length measurement, varying from one province to the next, causing great difficulties in domestic and foreign trade that made it quite difficult, particularly for children to learn. These were abandoned and the metric system put into effect throughout Turkey.[15]

(4) Replacement of National Wearing Tradition;

Ataturk replaced the old fashioned National wearing tradition with the western type dresses and hats. So the external view of Turkish people was changed, too.[16]

e. Economic Strategy of Ataturk

As the person who planned and carried out important social and political reforms and revolutions, Ataturk did not neglect to support his program with an applicable economic foundation. The Kemalist economic development model had unique characteristics which could set an example for underdeveloped nations of the world, just as in the example he had set for political and social independence for these nations. He formed his own economic ideology over the years and applied it throughout his era. This economic ideology was based on the following basic concepts:

1. Establish obvious and measurable "goals and vehicles." To obtain the economic development Ataturk used a systems approach, harmonizing these vehicles aimed at achieving these goals, and results that could be shown and measured within the subsystems, and a feedback mechanism for adjusting the actual performance in cases of variations from pre-determined goals. Ataturk explained the systems approach he applied to the economic and social development of Turkish society as follows:

"The national economy should be viewed as a whole. Agricultural, commercial, and industrial activities, and all public works are part of a whole; to think of them independent from each other is inappropriate. I should remind you that in the social machine, which gives a nation independent identity and esteem, the mechanisms of the state, intellect and economy are interconnected and dependent on each other; so much so that if these mechanisms are not synchronized, the locomotive force of the government machinery is wasted and the expected complete efficiency is not obtained."[17]

2. Ataturk accepted state intervention in the economy, but gave paramount importance to protection of personal wealth, initiative, and freedom. In his own words;

"The system of stateism applied in Turkey is not a system interpreted from the ideas which the socialist theorists have proposed since the nineteenth century. It stems from the needs of Turkey; it is a system unique to Turkey. Stateism means this to us: to keep private enterprise as the most important economic base, however, to have a state-controlled economy, considering all the needs of this large nation and spacious country, and all the things yet to be done."[18]

Ataturk indicated that to reach the goals stated and to achieve unity of action in the society with the systems approach discussed in his own words above, the following strategies should be applied:

(a) To achieve prosperity and a fair distribution of income, privileged groups or classes in any sector of the society should be prevented; the products of development should be equally distributed to all sectors, classes, and groups.

(b) The economy should be managed according to the rules of market economy in the supervision and direction of markets, and in direct industrial and trade projects the state should obey the rules of the market economy.

(c) The power of private enterprise should be protected and supported. In his own words:

"Private initiative and free enterprise should be preserved as the base in economic development, and this is only natural.
Furthermore, the acceptance of this basic rule is in turn the basic condition for preserving democracy and the most effective way of speeding up economic and social development."[19]

(d) The state should watch over and supervise the field of private enterprise and encourage its direction towards basic economic goals.

(e) To prevent barriers to free enterprise, it was very important to establish limits for the direct investments of the state, and the role and importance of the state's control of the economy. These limits, because of the dynamics of economic life, could not be rigid and inflexible. One of the main duties of the government should be to review these limits from time to time and adjust them.

(f) Investments in the economic substructure which were suitable for state companies and enterprises should have top priority in the list for government investments. The priorities of the state's basic duties should not be forgotten while the state makes investment expenditures in the economic field. These priorities as listed by Ataturk are briefly as follows:

(I) Achieving public order and peace in the country.

(II) National defense and foreign affairs.

(III) Transportation.

(IV) National Education.

(V) Health.

(VI) Social Security.

(VI) Economic activities related to agriculture, trade, and arts and crafts.

f. The Fundamental Policies To Support the Economic Strategies.

To reach the goals of the economic strategies, Ataturk established a series of policies based on balanced development in the economic area. These are as follows:

(1) A Balanced State Budget.

(2) A Balance between Sources and Expenditures on the GNP

(3) A Balance between Foreign Income and Expenditures.

(4) A Balance between Private and Government Business Enterprises.

The results of implementation of these strategies and policies, during the 74 years of the Republic, the 15-year (1923-1938) Ataturk era was the period of the economy's most steady and rapid development.

IV. CONCLUSION

As I mentioned before, Ataturk's first aim was the establishment of a national state. Just after the Independence War, Ataturk started the fundamental revolutions for modernizing Turkey. The new Turkish state, founded in 1920, required a new legal system. Ataturk adopted the Swiss Civil Code as a substitute for canonical law (theological law), and substituted the penal code then in force with the Italian Penal Code. Hence the Turkish legal system was modernized consistent with the contemporary requirements. As a result of this modification, secularism, one of the fundamentals of Ataturk's revolutions, signifying the complete separation of government and religious affairs, was adopted.

Until the beginning of the nineteenth century, several educational systems pervaded in the Ottoman Empire. Ataturk observed that such systems dominant at Muslim theological schools, did not meet the needs of the society. It was essential to establish a new educational system similar to the western models. Thus, the existing system was changed. In 1933, a university reform was introduced.

One of the most important of Ataturk's reforms was the abolition of the use of the Arabic script and the adoption of the Latin script. In 1928, the new Turkish alphabet was adopted.

Following the revolution on the script, which was meant to be a kind of nationalism in the cultural field, Ataturk concentrated his attention on history. He established the Turkish Historical Society in 1931. Here, Turkey's historical past was thoroughly examined and evaluated.

With the Ataturk's reforms, Turkish women, who for centuries had been left neglected, were given new rights. Thus, with the civil code passed, Turkish women would enjoy equal rights with those of the men, could be appointed to official posts, would enjoy the right to vote and to be elected to the parliament. The monogamy principle and equal rights for women changed the spirit of the society. With the reform on dress, women stopped wearing veils and men started to wear western style garb.

Between 1924-1936, many other reforms had been achieved other than those already mentioned. As an example, in 1924 the Weekend Act, in 1925 International Time and Calendar system, in 1926 Obligation Law and Commercial Law, in 1933 System of Measures keeping with the western standards, and in 1934 the Surname Act.

As a result of the revolutions, the westernization of Turkey became easier, and Turkey's economic structure was completely changed for the better. With the annulment of capitulations, fundamentals needed to secure a national and liberal economy, were achieved. Ataturk's foreign policy is based on, as he himself had underlined, "Peace at Home, Peace in the World."

In today's world countries are experiencing circumstances similar to those which Turkey had before Ataturk's revolutions, and therefore are open to communist influences. Therefore, the social, economic, and political revolutions accomplished in Turkey during the Ataturk era clearly demonstrate what can be done in third world countries to promote development and counter communist influences. Ataturk proved it can be done!

Endnotes

[1]Muzaffer Erendil, <u>Cok Yonlu Lider Ataturk</u> (Ankara Turkey: Gnkur, Basimevi, 1986), 118.

[2] Ibid.,82.

[3] Lt Col Ercument Tomak, <u>Ataturk's Strategic Approach to the Modernization of Turkey</u> (U.S. Air Force Air University, Maxwell Air Force Base, AL, 1988), 4.

[4] Ibid., 5.

[5] Ibid., 6.

[6] Muzaffer Erendil, <u>Cok Yonlu Lider Ataturk</u> (Ankara Turkey: Gnkur, Basimevi, 1986), 244.

[7] Ibid., 63.

[8] Ibid., 145.

[9] Ibid., 160.

[10] Ahmet Koklugiller, <u>Nutuk</u> (Istanbul Turkey, Milliyet Yayinlari, 1981), 167.

[11] Office of the Ambassador for Cultural Affiars, Republic of Turkey, <u>Ataturk. Creator of Modern Turkey</u> (UN Plaza New York, NY: Office of the Ambassador for Cultural Affairs, 1981), 11.

[12] Ibid., 12.

[13] Ibid., 11.

[14] Ibid., 8.

[15] Ibid., 13.

[16] Ibid.

[17] Lt Col Ercument Tomak, <u>Ataturk's Strategic Approach to the Modernization of Turkey</u> (U.S. Air Force Air University, Maxwell Air Force Base, AL, 1988), 12.

[18] Ibid., 17.

[19] Ibid., 18.

BIBLIOGRAPHY

1. Turkiye Cumhuriyeti Genelkurmay Baskanligi, <u>Ataturk</u>, Ankara, 1981.

2. Erendil, Muzaffer, Em. Tumg. <u>Cok Yonlu Lider Ataturk,</u> Ankara, 1986.

3. Tokmak, Ercument, <u>Ataturk's strategic approach to the modernization of Turkey</u>, U.S. AIR WAR COLLEGE, ALABAMA, 1988.

4. Office of the Ambassador for Cultural Affairs, Republic of Turkey, Turkish Center, <u>Ataturk, Creator of Modern Turkey</u>, New York, 1981.

5. Yilmaz , Veli, Dr. Kur. Alb. <u>Ataturk ilkeleri ve inkilaplari,</u> Istanbul, 1993.

6. Tezer, Sukru, <u>Ataturk'un hatira defteri,</u> Ankara, 1972.

7. Koklugiller, Ahmet, <u>Nutuk,</u> Istanbul, 1981.